STRENGTH of SPIRIT

by Halima Hadavi

Editorial Offices: Glenview, Illinois • Parsippany, New Jersey • New York, New York
Sales Offices: Needham, Massachusetts • Duluth, Georgia • Glenview, Illinois
Coppell, Texas • Sacramento, California • Mesa, Arizona

Helen Keller

Franklin D. Roosevelt

Imagine if you fell down and broke your leg. You couldn't play soccer or ride a bicycle. You might even have to use a wheelchair to move around. Some people are lucky and live their lives without any physical injury. But many people face physical challenges of different kinds—loss of sight or hearing, not being able to walk, or not being able to use their legs or arms.

Let's meet two people with disabilities who achieved extraordinary things. They were born around the same time, and later in life they were friends: Helen Keller and Franklin D. Roosevelt. Both became famous for what they did rather than something they could not do.

---

disabilities: physical or mental conditions that limit one or more activities, such as walking, seeing, hearing, and the like

Helen Keller
(1880–1968)

    Helen Keller was born in Tuscumbia, Alabama. Helen was not yet two years old when she became very ill. She had a very high fever. Doctors did not know what was wrong, but her illness left her deaf and blind. She could not hear or see. Her life was one of silence and darkness. She had to use her hands to feel her mother's and father's faces so that she could recognize them.

    At the age of seven, Helen's behavior was uncontrollable. She would scream and break things. Her parents allowed her to act this way. Yet they knew something had to be done to help her.

---

fever: rise in body temperature above normal

Annie helped Helen learn words by spelling them on Helen's hand.

Helen's parents hired a teacher named Annie Sullivan. Annie also had problems with her vision. Annie moved in with the Keller family and began to help Helen communicate. She wanted to teach Helen language by using finger spelling. Annie would use her fingers to spell into Helen's hand. At first, Helen would repeat the hand movements that Annie used, but Helen did not understand that Annie was spelling words. Annie would spell C-A-K-E and give Helen a piece of cake, but Helen did not make the connection between the word that Annie spelled and the cake.

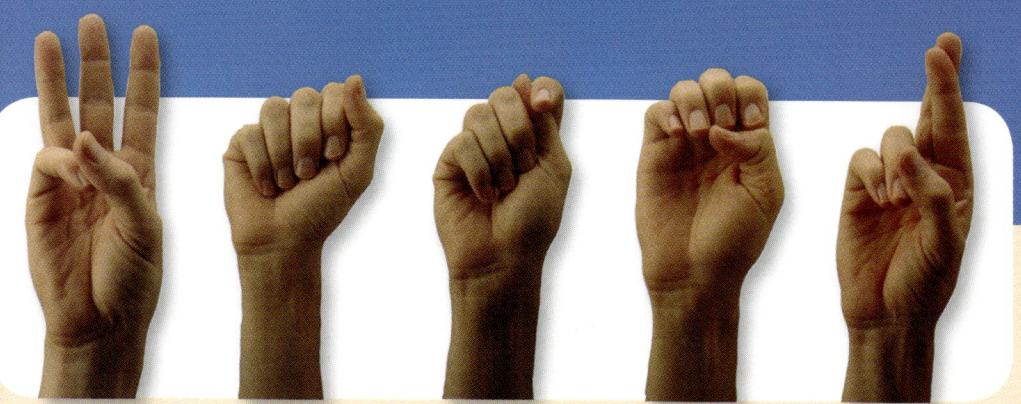

These finger shapes spell the word *water*.

Annie spent a month spelling into Helen's hands and working with her to control her temper. Then a wonderful event took place. Annie took Helen to the water pump to get water. As the cold water flowed over one of Helen's hands, Annie spelled W-A-T-E-R over and over again into her free hand. Then Helen spelled the word back! In that moment, Helen understood the idea of language. Helen was very excited and began touching things and holding out her hand. She wanted Annie to spell the names of these things to her.

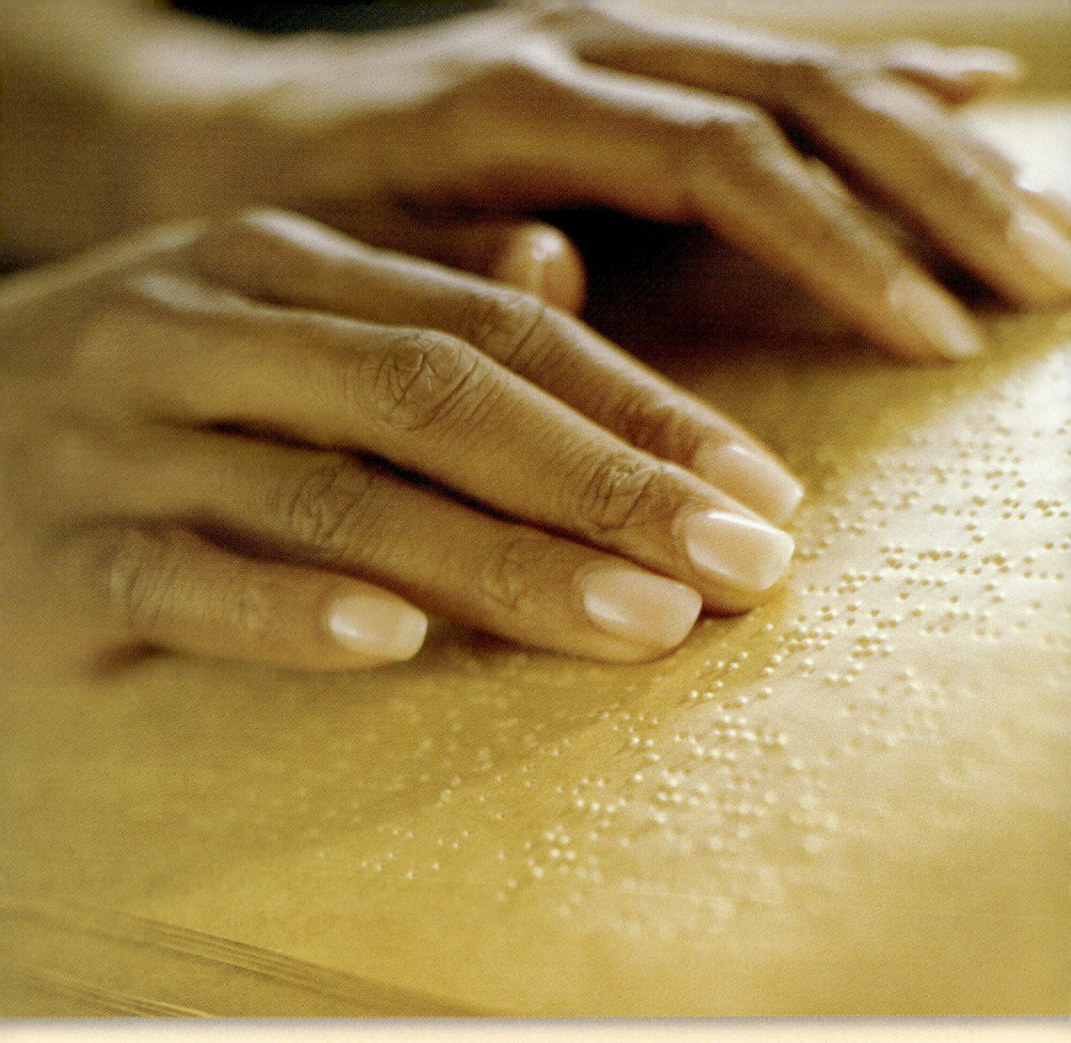

Braille is a system of writing that uses dots to be read by people with poor eyesight or who are blind.

The day Helen realized that objects had names was the beginning of her new life. Helen was a fast learner, and she started learning things that other school children learned. She studied math and read stories. Annie would either read the stories to Helen by spelling into her hand, or Helen would use Braille. Books that are in Braille have patterns of raised dots that represent letters. Blind people use Braille to read by feeling the dots.

Helen Keller and Annie Sullivan

At the age of 20, Helen became the first deaf and blind person to attend Radcliffe College. Annie attended school with Helen, to help her study and read. While in college, Helen began writing her first book, *The Story of My Life*.

When Helen graduated from Radcliffe, she moved in with Annie and Annie's husband. Helen traveled with Annie, talking to audiences about her experiences. Helen would always call attention to the need for education for deaf and blind people. Helen would sign into Annie's hand, and Annie would speak to each audience. During this time, Helen also wrote many articles, essays, and books. In her lifetime, she wrote eleven books. Helen also appeared in a few movies about her life.

Helen Keller with President Calvin Coolidge, 1926

When Helen was not traveling or writing, she was raising money for the American Foundation for the Blind. During the early 1900s, blind people often were sent to institutions. These places did not offer the kind of care and support that blind people needed. Helen was upset that blind people were not educated and wanted to change that. Helen traveled all over the world to help blind and deaf people.

Because of her fame, Helen met twelve U.S. presidents. She wrote letters to President Franklin Roosevelt for many years. Like Helen Keller, President Roosevelt also overcame physical disabilities.

---

institutions: places organized for special purposes, such as homes where people live and are cared for

Franklin Delano Roosevelt
(1882–1945)

Franklin Delano Roosevelt was born in New York. He was an only child who liked to swim, sail, and collect stamps. After he graduated from college, he decided to become a politician. He entered the race to become a senator in the New York state senate, and he won. Everything in his life was wonderful until the summer of 1921.

He was at his summer home on Campobello Island. He spent the day sailing, swimming, and jogging—all the things he loved to do. That night, Roosevelt did not feel well. He thought he was just tired. When he awoke the next morning, his legs ached, and he had a high fever. He told doctors he had no feeling in his back, arms, and legs. He had been ill before, but this was serious.

---

ached: were in pain

At first his doctors thought he had the flu or a spinal injury—an injury to his backbone. But weeks later, a doctor told him he had polio.

Polio is a disease caused by a virus. The virus enters the body through the mouth and attacks the brain and spinal cord. It causes muscle weakness and paralysis. Polio is more common in children than in adults, but at age 39 Roosevelt had polio. He was never able to walk without help again.

---

paralysis: loss of movement or feeling in parts of the body

Franklin Delano Roosevelt gave radio speeches, giving hope to millions of citizens.

But Roosevelt was a fighter. He did not keep his disease a secret, but he did try to hide it. There were many Americans who had no idea that Roosevelt was crippled by the disease—unable to use his legs. Yet, Roosevelt wanted to help those who were disabled. He purchased land in Warm Springs, Georgia, and opened the Georgia Warm Springs Foundation in 1927. The land had a spring or natural pool with warm, healing waters. Since its opening, it has developed many treatments and tools to help disabled people.

In 1928, Roosevelt became the Governor of New York. Then, in 1933, he became the President of the United States. The country was suffering through difficult financial times, and Roosevelt offered people jobs, financial aid, and hope. When the United States faced World War II, Roosevelt was a strong leader for the United States and for the world.

Helen Keller's books are still popular today.

To honor Roosevelt, the United States government placed an image of his face on the dime in 1946.

President Roosevelt also created the National Foundation for Infantile Paralysis. He wanted to find a cure for polio. A friend suggested that he should call the organization the March of Dimes and ask each American to send in a dime. It did not take long before the White House was full of dimes. Millions of dollars went into finding a cure. By 1955, the vaccine for polio was approved.

Strength of Spirit

Helen Keller and Franklin D. Roosevelt both had strength of spirit. Both were determined individuals with their own dreams and challenges. They fought for improvements in living conditions, employment, and research. They were able to change the public's attitude toward the handicapped. Their strength of spirit made a difference.

---

vaccine: a kind of medicine used to prevent a disease